ROUNDABOUT

Roundabout

POEMS

Amy M. Clark

Press 53
Winston-Salem

Press 53, LLC
PO Box 30314
Winston-Salem, NC 27130

First Edition

Copyright © 2020 by Amy M. Clark

All rights reserved, including the right of reproduction in whole or in part in any form except in the case of brief quotations embodied in critical articles or reviews. For permission, contact publisher at editor@Press53.com, or at the address above.

Cover Art, "vintage tone image of old carousel day time," by BLUR LIFE 1975. Licensed through Shutterstock.

Author Photo, Mira Whiting Photography

Cover design, Christopher Forrest and Kevin Morgan Watson

Library of Congress Control Number
2020933881

Printed on acid-free paper
ISBN 978-1-950413-20-1

For Jonah

Many thanks to the editors of the following journals, where versions of these poems first appeared:

The Cape Rock, "Your Husband"

Cave Wall, "Roundabout"

Cloudbank, "Now Approaching Porter Square"

The Cresset, "Armed" and "Excused"

FUSION, "Elegy for Our Dog"

The Louisville Review, "My Son's Abandoned Aquarium" and "The New Winter"

Southern Humanities Review, "Belongs To"

Southern Poetry Review, "The Bluest Lake," "Going Back," and "Thin Chain"

The poems "An Answer," "Belongs To," and "The Bluest Lake" are included in the chapbook *A Turn Around the Mansion Grounds: Poems in Conversation & A Conversation*, co-authored with Molly Peacock, Slapering Hol Press, 2014.

A warmest thank you to Christopher Forrest for shepherding this book into publication with a keen eye and generous spirit, and to Kevin Morgan Watson, Tom Lombardo, and all at Press 53. For supporting this work and me in the making of it, bouquets of appreciation to Tom Berriman, Brian Burt, Debra Kang Dean, Jennifer S. Flescher, Joan Houlihan and the Colrain Poetry Manuscript Conference, Kirun Kapur, Ron McAdow, Richard Newman, Cecily Parks, Molly Peacock, Mike Perrow, Beth Woodcome Platow, Christine Portell, Kevin Prufer, Glenn Stowell, Cammy Thomas, Erin Trahan, Rhett Iseman Trull, Kate Westhaver, Leslie Williams, and Scott Withiam. A special thank you to Lynne Potts for the Saturday group and so much more. Love and thank you always to my family, to Jonathan Weinert, and with all my heart to Jonah Weinert.

Contents

On Our Street We Don't Understand What We're Seeing	3
Armed	4
Spotless	6
The Newest Baby	7
Impression	8
Roundabout	9
Stupid	10
An Answer	11
I Called It Beautiful and Lost It	12
Belongs To	13
Runner on a Winter Night	14
Triolet for My Son	15
Sea Glass	16

*

Going Back	19
The Bluest Lake	20
Family Friend	21
Charges	22
Leah and Val	23
The Babysitter	24
The Professor's Bathroom	25
Rounds	26
The Thing Is to Stay Busy	28
Excused	29
Unlikely	30
The Vase Had a Fluted Rim and Was Probably Meant to Add a Splash of Color	31
Triolet for My Son	32
In Alaska	33

*

Elsewhere	37
Two in a House	38
Parent Pick-Up	39
Division Street	40
Roosting	41
One Act	42
Thin Chain	43
Elegy for Our Dog	44
The Survival Kit	45
Triolet for My Son	46
Passers by a Wedding	47

The New Winter	51
Single Again in Middle Age	52
My Son's Abandoned Aquarium	53
Your Husband	54
Now Approaching Porter Square	55
Arrangements	56
Boys on the Lake Dock	57
Aerialist, Sixteen	58
The Wong-Baker FACES Pain Rating Scale	59
To the Mother of the Family That Moved In	60
Going up to Sleep in the Late Afternoon	61
The Joy Spell	62
Triolet for My Son	63
About the Author	65

Roundabout

On Our Street We Don't Understand What We're Seeing

Every kitchen blackens toast. Cats cross back and forth.
        Snow shovels stowed, we step out of doors, trundling

the newest babies. From yard to yard, they exercise button eyes
        while the toddler boys maintain their toy-truck inventories.

Beside yellow Children Playing signs, I do my part to call out "Car!"
        and nod to slowing neighbors. With its turret

and wrap-around porch, the ochre house was the stateliest.
        Last year we watched the renovations, then strolled down

the stone path to a garden party. Now, after the break-up, a realtor
        embeds her sign in the wild lawn. I wonder if our walls

fell away, and I peered through scaffolding from house to house,
        clear down the street, would I recognize a friend?

ARMED

Sprung to Atlantic air, a boy.
Show him your face, bring him
your smell. Feed him your milk.
Already he seeks your pleasure.
Clap for him. You give it.

*

Today my baby would not sleep.
He arched and fought within himself,
careening from fatigue.
I secured him in his infant seat
and drove through bedroom towns
until he nodded off. And even then
I stayed the course, past mailboxes,
maple woods, election signs,
and mounds of rotting leaves,
propelled by public radio,
half asleep myself, at least
not carrying anything, not singing.

I thought of stopping at a general store,
going inside, floorboards creaking.
I'd drink a cup of coffee while browsing
through the postcard rack,
just a gal thinking of someone
to send a message to
or not, while locked in the car my son—

*

Fast asleep. And I, scaring
out of reverie, still driving.
Then I heard the news.
Somewhere not far from here—
as everywhere was not too far
—at the Machine Gun Shoot
and Firearms Expo, Christopher,
age eight, aimed and fired
a 9mm micro submachine gun
at a pumpkin, and while his dad reached
for a camera, the gun recoiled and the boy
lost control, shooting himself in the head.

I pulled into a parking lot
and craned to view my passenger,
his eyelids without a flutter.
He held a yellow plastic bale of hay
he'd chosen from his farm set,
the rounded shape just right
for his untrained palm, discovering
the pleasure in having something to keep.

*

Or so I decided, and let him hold it,
because it was my pleasure, after all,
in a small and cherished thing,
small enough to swallow, actually,
but large enough to lodge in the throat—
and what would I say to his father
when my car came home without him,
the world fallen from my hands.

Spotless

I can count only on apologies. I'm sorry
my house is a mess. Oh please, you should see mine.
I've lived here, what, nine years? You'd think
I'd have that latch fixed by now. I can count only
on admissions of failure. I didn't send cards this year.
I meant to. People will understand. Will they?
Why are we worried? I hope I didn't come at a bad time.
Is this a bad time? I just wanted to return your pan.
After scrubbing it, I put it in the dishwasher.
I hope that's all right. It's fine. That's much cleaner
than I've ever managed. And it's true. The baking pan
my neighbor borrowed came back spotless,
without the grease stains I'd grown accustomed to.
I pictured my neighbor at her kitchen sink,
energetically scouring my Pyrex, shaking her head.

The Newest Baby

There's a new baby living across the street.
I've just heard. Ninety-eight degrees on the outside thermometer.
No activity in front of the house. Air conditioner
wedged in an upstairs window. Drawn shade.

How can we shield a new baby's eyes?
In each house we've done what was needed. The milk
sprang forth. We'll knock on the latest door, bringing
our meals, our big shapes, our explanations.

Nighttime of the third day my son would not stop crying.
His father took him from me into the car.
Raccoon feet on the roof. Train rattling the frame.
I couldn't soothe him. These thick sheets

of hot rain. Sometimes they swaddle, sometimes smother
my terror, my apologies, my being like everyone else.

Impression

Smoothing sheets, I made the beds
and dressed my boy in neon shorts,

the ones he'd begged to have. Outside
when I yanked him from the road, he bit me.

Teeth clamped on my forearm, he drove
his indignation in. Fierce badger.

Unable to budge him, I bloomed into dark
purple and held on while his teeth made

their imprint and engines and birds sped past.
Then he let go and I looked into his face.

"You didn't have to grab me by the wrist!"
he cried, as if across a great rift. "Yes

I did!" I shouted back from the other side
where all I could do was watch it grow.

Roundabout

The guard tower is a clock, a cockpit, a woman's hat.
Giant wire hair rollers line the chain-link fence. I've entered
the nearby rotary after adult ballet class. Out there

in the yellow-lit dark, *it's as cold as a witch's tit.*
An ex-lover used to say that. I wouldn't.
Muscle memory doesn't fail me. I make the same mistakes

I made when I was eight, like looking down before
my *grand jeté*. Two women and a child are leaving the prison
again. The woman on the left carries the baby girl on her hip,

and the taller, larger woman carries the purses.
The baby girl on the hip bumps along. Past her bedtime,
past her bedtime. I'm going around another time

and the trio continues, slowly down the icy walk.
The women bend into the wind. Baby's got on a pink parka,
dirty white boots. One pant leg is hitched up under Mama's arm,

exposing some bare skin—something I always ache to correct—
whatever mother, whatever child, in whatever cold.

Stupid

Back-to-back doors between the rooms lock
on each side and let the noises through.

Stupid, a boy is told in that room. *Stupid*, I tell
myself in this room. We're in the stupid rooms.

It's snowing in March, and it's hard to name
the color of the walls and the bedspread.

Last week, I compromised myself again. What
is the thudding against that door? *Stop*.

Say it. Say you're stupid, you little shit.
Shit. *Don't be a crybaby. You baby.*

*

What did you see?
A boy in a snowsuit, the security guard replied.

The kid said his dad was in the shower. The TV was on.
The shower has the slippery slice of soap.

I didn't pack my snowsuit, long outgrown.
It isn't my business.

My business is in this room
putting a name in its place.

An Answer

I couldn't answer your question
"Why do we exist?" except with the non-answer
"I don't know." You charged at me in tears.

"You don't understand!" You wanted
an answer you could follow with another question,
as in, "Where did I come from?"

"You came from your dad and me." "But where did *you*
come from?" "We came from *our* parents."
Until you ask, "But how did the first person get here?"

Bacteria, you say, are neither good nor bad.
They are just living their lives. I thought of this
when your teacher told me you said "Fuck" at circle time

after the principal announced that recess was canceled.
And then your best friend tried it out. "Fuck."
Likely the word ricocheted through each six-year-old head.

On the way home, you said from the back seat,
"I'm suddenly crying and I don't know why."
I turned to look. You were small and strapped in.

But you told me your tears were not from anything
you were feeling inside. "You mean your eyes are watering?"
I asked. You wanted to know what the difference was.

I Called It Beautiful and Lost It

Recalling his first sound requires my eyes
closing rendering myself hospital-gowned
clearing this space of all that belies
      recalling his sound

like paper snowflakes I cut around
unfolding each imprecise surprise
not quite right not quite found

I see I see even the dimples of his thighs
but his first clear coos have drowned
and even my farthest reach denies
      recalling his sound

Belongs To

Share. It gets so tiresome.

Does my son really have to hand over his shovel
to whoever shows up wanting a turn?

Yet I fault the mother in the park who snatches
her pink tennis ball out of his hands and goes on
gabbing into her phone.

The peas he planted in preschool take root
in the child-sized pot labeled with his name.

No! he wails. I don't want us to have
Grandma Lois's table. I like *our* dining room table.
He hugs its crippled leg.

Grandma Lois faces decisions about her dinnerware.
To me she bequeaths a lidded white and black bowl.
Gustavsberg, she says. It's worth something.

Riding in the front seat, the dish is a small child
without a booster. My arm shoots out when I brake.

I place the bowl on our broken table. I rest
my eyes on the clean form
until I love it.

Runner on a Winter Night

Here you come,
runner of my evening
commute, as consistent
as the leaning mailbox,
the long wait
at the Route 27 stoplight,
the corner graveyard,
and the red revolving
dashboard numbers.

Here you come
through the record-breaking
cold, the rest of us warm,
hungry for home.

Here you come
on the road's frozen shoulder
in your panther clothes,
neon sparking off your shoes,
your tears whipped sideways.

Why can't you skip tonight?
Who is counting on you?

Triolet for My Son

I've been your mother for a decade
and keep a pinecone on the sill—
There's not one bit I'd trade
for other luck. You, my son for a decade,
have loved a dog, a blanket, a game you made.
Now, holding back my kisses is an act of will.
I've been your mother for a decade
and keep a pinecone on the sill.

Sea Glass

I could be the sort who combs low tide
for rounded glass, big dog romping at my side,

long hair, long skirt, lace-trimmed T-shirt, a grace
as, bent at the waist, I pluck trifles I'll place

on window sills and drop in bowls, my claim
to loving bottle green, depression blue, the tame

rare shipwrecked orange. You've seen me, yes?
Petted my dog? Arranging my duress,

my ease, in scavenged bits, altered, weathered,
I still myself, as do all things tethered.

*

Going Back

Sometimes you have to go back
        for the thing you've forgotten
                that you cannot do without—
      all that remains
of the food, or your notebook. So
        you turn back, an act of subtraction,
                hoping the thing is still there
      unimportant
to anyone but you. Your head is down.
        You keep a horse's pace: *I'm going*
                back, I hope it's there, back I go,
      have to, have to.
You pass the places you saw for the first time
        going forward, lusterless now, peripheral.
                Usually, a person gets in the way.
        And years go by.
Somewhere—you know exactly where—
        you wait, hunched and quiet,
                a stone figure in a garden
        collecting rain.

The Bluest Lake

They said envision what you love. Cold lake,
blue room. It would be over soon. Undressed,
I swam although my chest began to ache,
then climbed a mica-glinting rock to rest
until the sliding sun's unfurling sash
laid out a dreamway to the western shore
and light-reflecting waves held up a cache
of pinwheels, pirouetting gems, before
the shadow of the eastern ridge reclaimed
my cove. No use, I thought of you. (Suppose
we'd never met.) Recovering's well named.
They sat me up and handed me my clothes.
Clouds traversed a distant dab of blue.
Bright. Then dark. A last, indifferent hue.

Family Friend

Comes for dinner. Cooks a chicken.
Dominates the conversation.
Flops down on the fold-out bed.
Tackles us, makes me giggle.

Family rules go out the door.
Leads us girls through coastal woods
adorns our hair with wildflowers,
mission bells and fiddlenecks.

Captures us with a zoom. Taller
than my dad and brother. He's
anti-nuke beside my mother.
How he makes her laugh and beam.

If she's happy, so am I.
I'm so brave and I'm so different.
I'm so strong and independent.
While my friends go to class,

I'm the girl who gets to drift
in no more than a 10-foot raft
down the Río Santiago.
Moonlit cliffs. Thorny sand.

His hands sneak in my sleeping bag.
"Don't," I say, not at once.
Morning breaks. I'm not all here.
I check my shoes for scorpions.

Charges

My sister,
younger by one scant year,
tucked her daughters in
and flew the red-eye from L.A. to Boston
ahead of the spring rains. Here:
my newborn son. He takes
to her expert arms. Mine fall to my sides
like a sigh.

Growing up,
we shared a bedroom. My sister asleep
was as common as a glass of milk.
I didn't listen for her cry or think about
all the things that could go wrong
when our parents turned their backs.
To me she had no need or want beyond
our nightly exchange—
"I'm turning my light out."
"Ok. Do you mind if I keep reading?"

They fall asleep—
baby changed and swaddled in his crib,
sister on the sofa, true-crime story
she'd nearly finished over Pennsylvania
opened on her chest. She'd been telling me
about the dash-cam playback,
the state trooper forced to kneel
at gunpoint by the highway,
praying "Jesus loves me" before the shot.
In the stillness, I listen to the leaves.

Leah and Val

There were two girls who liked me for my brother—
the wrong girls. Leah was *retarded*. She'd call to me
from the high school's front steps, "Say hi to Jim,"

sweet as pink cake. For one Saturday, I agreed
to be her buddy at the regional Special Olympics.
I put it on my college application. The other girl

was from earlier. I was eleven and Val was twelve
with breasts. At my house, we watched my brother
work on his model cars, his desk lined with jars

of metallic colors. Val put her face in his pillow
and prowled his room, touching things. In her house
the only light came from *The Beverly Hillbillies*,

a show I didn't like. She told me to ask my mom
if I could spend the night. She showed me where to feel
her body with my hands. For breakfast we ate pancakes

but I can't recall who made them, though I slept over
more than once. When my father took a new job
we moved away, as if that were the only possible end.

The Babysitter

At the end of the evenings, the husbands paid me
and drove me home. I sat in the wife seat
next to Mr. Vance, Mr. Aiken, or Mr. Gordon,
hugging my schoolbooks, worried about what to say.

These days on the treadmill in the gym, a strong beat
pounding in my ears, I'm running across a cool desert at dusk.
I'm running not for fitness, but to reach somewhere distant,
to deliver a message or medicine, my hair streaming behind me.

Sometimes we talked about the children's activities.
Sometimes they asked about my classes.
In front of my house, I blurted, *Thank you*, and hurried
up the walk while they saw that I got inside, then pulled away.

Mile after loping mile, bared muscles
and ticking breath turbo-charging through soreness,
I'm sleeker, smarter, faster, a deep, growling engine,
every nerve a wide-throated yellow monkey flower.

They were just men, no different from those I know now.
Making their decisions, pulling on their socks, roaming
their houses. Their hands along the wheel, the hairs
on the backs of their fingers, their rocky throats.

The Professor's Bathroom

At the professor's party
in one of the tract homes
along the ridge, I went
into a little bathroom
under the stairs and latched
the door. I had stepped
into another country.
The walls and slanting ceiling,
painted hot pink, were adorned
with woodblock prints of birds,
women, and music notes.
The floor tiles sparkled
with turquoise and silver
mosaic fish. A warm
toilet seat surprised
and then delighted me.
On a stand by the wash basin
a basket of striped soaps
filled the room with an aroma
of bergamot, lemon, and vanilla.
My eyes looked large and multiple
in a tin-framed, fold-out mirror.
I'd been up all night to complete
my final paper on *L'Allegro*
and *Il Penseroso*. I didn't think I knew
what I was talking about.
The professor had translated
The Arabian Nights. He liked
to remind us there is nothing new
under the sun. Standing
before the mirror in his spectacular
bathroom, I saw how anything
can be made into something other.

Rounds

He had a gun. He wasn't a bad man
and in his heart he wished no one harm
although he harbored ill will
toward his first wife, his boss, and a few others.
He had a gun, his father had guns,
and his father's father had guns.
His was a 9mm Glock. At one time
he also had two rifles, but he gave them away,
one to each of his sons, now young men
who took the rifles to their own homes.

He kept the gun, unloaded, in a case
under a pile of folded t-shirts on a shelf
in the closet of the bedroom he shared
with his second wife. There was
a box of bullets somewhere. They lived
their lives and the gun was a piece of metal
shaped like a gun. They loved each other
not without difficulty. You could say
the gun slept, or hibernated. Or
you might say it lay in wait, fully alert.

He drank and became desperate
to keep hold of his wife, not because
he thought it best for them but because
he couldn't see another way. Now
he brought the gun from its case.
His wife saw him come down the hall
holding the gun to his head. Even as he did so
he wished the gun back in its case,
even as he knocked her down
and as he took the gun when he fled.

She did not press charges and sat with him
in the detox ward. She looked down
at his shoes, stripped of their laces.
She'd found the box of 50 rounds intact.
You might say this story is not over
because after all the gun has not been fired,
and maybe you're right. Now the gun
rests in its case in the older son's home,
in the manner of all weapons,
or in the manner of women and men.

The Thing Is to Stay Busy

Once in the Old Clam House
while we prepared for the dinner rush
a waiter placed two full water glasses
on the backs of my hands
and left me standing in front of the bread

Each day I observe
how water keeps at it, evaporating

Excused

After my son
finished eating and left
the table, taking his plate
to the kitchen, I remained
sitting with the bunched-up
napkins, the salt
and pepper shakers,
empty salad bowl,
and milk-rimmed glass.
I pushed my own plate
to the side. I put
my head down
and cradled it
with my arms. This

was familiar. This body
like this was familiar.
This weight in here. This
muting. It was

my father, after dinner
at the table of six.
We scraped our plates
around him and went off
to do our homework
or lessons. Talk
on the phone. Change
shoe sizes. Fill out
applications. Starve
ourselves. Marry.
Receive our rewards.

Unlikely

It was like any other day
when she woke.
She washed her hair
and chose her clothes.
She didn't know she was leaving
the earth. I shouldn't
have had anything to do
with her tonight.
After reading her name,
in memoriam, on our 25th
reunion homepage, after
I learn she was shot
by her ex-husband
and I study the picture of her,
her same-age face,
I begin to google people
I care about. I find my ex-stepson
playing the hell out of a washboard
he wears around his neck.
I see his rolled-up plaid sleeves,
those tattoos along his forearms,
his hobo pants, black Fedora,
and how he taps his work boots
and sways, eyes toward the ceiling.
I see his busted-over, crooked nose,
and I don't care about the guy singing
or the guys on the upright bass
and lap steel guitar, only how,
strumming a washboard,
he lives through
the whole song and breaks out
a smile that looks damn gorgeous
just then, two years ago
at Evangeline's in Colfax.

The Vase Had a Fluted Rim and Was Probably Meant to Add a Splash of Color

Kneeling on the bathroom floor
down the hall from the therapist's office, I gathered
shards of a blue vase.

My big winter coat knocked it over.

Without gloves I can handle jagged glass.
The tiniest slivers
glinted under the radiator along the baseboards.
I wiped them up with a sheet of damp paper towel.

I left a note.

Triolet for My Son

I can't shield you from despair—
only try to build a little heat—
a gentle book, favorite chair,
pillowed fortress against despair,
round of tickles until you gasp for air—
and tuck the corners of this conceit.
I can't shield you from despair—
only try to build a little heat.

In Alaska

On Sunday mornings in our town's bakery café,
Chas and Linda Wood join Don and Gloria Stanhope.
They've known each other for years,
raised their kids together. Today at a table near mine,
the four huddle around a Kindle Fire
for a slideshow of Don and Gloria's Alaskan cruise.
Gloria taps through slides while Don narrates.
Mornings on deck, the Stanhopes enjoyed
eggs cooked to order and fresh pineapple.
Dolphin herds swam by as if on cue.
"*Pods*," Chas says. "Dolphin *pods*. Technically."
Linda lays a steadying hand on his arm.
Don powers on. At the port city of Ketchikan
the Stanhopes ventured off ship to view salmon runs
and look for black bears. "The fish were so exhausted,
you could reach in and grab one with your hands,"
Don announces. Gloria adds, "Easy prey for the bears."
"Is that brown thing a bear?" Chas asks, jabbing
his finger at the screen. Gloria laughs. "We never saw
a bear. That's a tree stump." Chas guffaws.
All lean back. "Stunning landscape," Linda offers.
Gloria concurs there's no place as pristine.
As they rise, Chas takes a last gulp from his mug
and glances in my direction. Have I been made?
Last week when the Stanhopes were away,
the Woods cozied on a sagging couch.
Linda read the *Globe*. Chas worked the crossword,
interrupting Linda to ask her the clues.
She usually knows the answers, and so do I.
In Alaska I've thought I would work hard
and serve my own needs. If I were hungry,
I would wrestle a fish from a stream.
If I were cold, I would skin a bear.
But if I were lonely, would I reveal myself?

Elsewhere

A week before your fiftieth birthday, we fought. We fought
so hard the salt dish skittered off the counter. I wish

I could say our baby slept while we fought, but he was there
turning his lovely head from me to you. That is the truth.

Maybe our fight offered a chance to observe how things work.
When a door closes hard and fast, it makes a loud sound.

We'll never know for sure. I'm glad we're on the same side
of the door. A rain drums while Jonah settles his little animals

into the laundry hamper and takes them out again. You and I
didn't have enough of getting into bed in the afternoon, lingering

through dusk and Chinese food. If I could order any day for you,
I'd wear heels, slipping one off to slide my toes along your calf

when we meet in the South End for a dirty martini. My longing
would remain, bottled so tightly it could never lose its kick.

Two in a House

It's beautiful. That place on the bed
that held his large ribcage
hers could fit inside.

The drops of her shower on the windowsill.

The picture frame that went askew
when he brushed by.

Days they filled their house but couldn't find each other
their bodies went on talking and touching
along temporary walkways.

Eastern white pines, old dog, order,
the minor key, him cooking for her.
When neither hesitated.

His coat nuzzled her coat on the kitchen chair.

Parent Pick-Up

Among the crush of cars
pulled to the curb, driven by mothers
detained in heated interiors,

a school van, stop sign out, lights flashing,
loaded a disabled child. It was I

who hummed past in the black Subaru,
intent on a parking spot.
The bus driver caught me

stepping out of my car
beside a mound of plowed snow.

"I've got your plate number," she barked
out her rolled-down window.
The child stuck out his tongue.

My mother was there in 1977
when another mother drove over a child

dragging him across wet asphalt
under the chassis.
My mother ran to help, her lab coat flying.

All I could see from our station wagon
was a wash of yellow and gray.

Even days
when I think I am trying my best
there is also everyone else.

Division Street

A modest house on a leafy street. Dad, Mom, children.
An accidental death. A house of irony, the newscasters imply.

"The gun didn't kill my son. I killed my son," the father says.
As if peering from behind parted curtains, I watch their driveway,

their wide front door, their bursting flowers in the wooden beds.
Sundays, they're dressed for church, then for the shooting range.

I wear orange to rallies. They'd be the first to help in time of need,
sending the girl with a casserole, the remaining boy to mow the lawn.

Roosting

The morning cartoons blaring,
Jonah's settled in the cozy chair
with his strawberries and waffle,
while the seven wild turkey poults
peck among the brush and needles
near the mudroom door. Yesterday
at dusk we saw their dark shapes
tucked up in the pine branches
without their mother, who'd been
sickly, our neighbor said. "But what
does a sickly turkey look like?"
Jonah asked, climbing into bed.
At 3 a.m. our smoke alarm erupted.
His father, flailing, yanked the thing
from the ceiling, shouting, "Shut up!
Shut up!" Dying battery.
Our son trembled in the hallway.
I lay down with him under the eaves,
pulling him under my arm, his dread
of a blast from his room's alarm
dissipating into sleep. Plush animals
tended from high on the shelves.
His father resumed snoring, a rumble.
Our luxury—shaken by a device
meant to protect us. And how easy
is it to feel sorry for a turkey?
They're doing fine. We're all fine.
Nothing happens. *Shut up, shut up*,
I told the circus that nattered on until
it was time to rise and warm the waffle iron.

One Act

"I can't find my wallet," he says, darkening the doorframe

where she is running a bath. She shuts off the faucet

and reaches for her robe. "No, don't stop what you're doing,"

he says. "I thought I could help you look," she says.

"I'm not asking for your help," he says. He goes away.

She hesitates, then puts her robe back on the hook

and steps into the water. She has a knack for finding things

often where he's already looked. But his problems are not hers

to fix. They've talked about that. Rummaging sounds

come from the kitchen. Yet it's ok to ask for help. They've talked

about that too. She thinks she knows where the wallet might be.

She could just go check on the floor by the bureau. She rises

from the bath and drips across the bedroom rug, but nothing is there.

Thin Chain

This night while you're away, I work
at untangling a silver chain necklace
here at the kitchen table. Before you went
you stocked the pantry with cereal, apples,
bread. I tug the line and nothing tugs back.

When I'd said our son spent his day pretending
to be someone else, you said, "Don't we all?"
You could be pouring yak butter into a lamp,
firelight across your jawbone. A gust of geese
flies over our yard. I'm making an effort.

If this part goes under this part, then this part
can get free from this part. Frogs clack
and cluck from the trees. The neighbor
steps out and makes noises, the clapping of shoes
to loosen wet grass. I've been holding my breath.

Elegy for Our Dog

This morning on waking
you and I were rolled to opposite edges
of our bed, as if trailing our hands
in the waters of two different oceans.

Last night I heard you
having a snack in the kitchen,
rinsing a plate, walking up the stairs.
I fell asleep before you reached me.

At the neighborhood cookout
we'd teased each other in the presence
of friends. Then momentarily
we were alone on the patio.

Our dog was allowed in our bedroom
but not on the bed. I miss her
nosing the mattress in the morning
and how I'd reach across you to pet her head.

The Survival Kit

In the days after we told you, and Dad moved out
leaving an empty bedroom that echoed your words
"I don't like the feeling here," the Emergency Survival Kit
you'd chosen from the Scholastic book order arrived.
It had a whistle, *to let your friends know where you are*,
a thermometer, a microscope, a compass, an LED light,
and a lanyard to wear the whole thing around your neck
for quick access when you are on the go. You tested the compass
in multiple rooms of our depleted house, and found
that the dial indicated North in the same direction
no matter where you stood. In those days after you began
to sometimes wake up in your same bed in our house
and go to sleep in your new bed in Dad's apartment,
twin 13-month-old boys conjoined at the head underwent
27 hours of surgery to be separated. You followed
their story on CNN checking for updates and studying
the videos showing their amazing before-and-after selves.
"You can do it, little guys," you whispered, as you saw each one
with bandaged head, breathing tube, IV, heart monitor,
and baby blanket, looking up from separate hospital cribs.
In the days after we told you, I became obsessed
with news about the impending election. Your dad said
if the wrong candidate won, we'd leave the country.
Oh, how I assured you we'd be fine. But relief was only
a flickering you have to gather all of your tools and wits to find.

Triolet for My Son

Which would you rather—
when either way, you lose.
Stay here and miss your father
or perhaps you would rather
live there and miss your mother.
Passed between us, you don't choose
which you would rather—
but either way, you lose.

Passers by a Wedding

While walking by the tiered
conservatory, you and I,
a bride and groom emerged.
She said to him, "We're married,"

the sparkling greenhouse glass
as backdrop. It cracked us up
how obvious. My happy day.
Are she and he, still, married?

*

The bag broke, rice spilled,
your broom ushered grains
across the floor, danced
them to the dustpan.

Come back. You missed
so many, scattered farther
than we thought. Sweep,
sweep again. Be certain.

*

White dogwood petals
splotched the red brick walk
along your street. I stood
before the house and tree

and took my vow, knowing
you weren't home, but the lamp
was, the vase was, and so was
the book signed to you and me.

*

At last. I've let go.
Because I kept you
in an email, I deleted it.
I kept you in a text. Gone.

I kept your image in a folder
that I trashed, then emptied
trash. I shut down. I quit
humming our favorite song.

The New Winter

It is a choice to summon you
to the window to glimpse the fox

cross the snow field and disappear
into the woods behind our house

and it's your choice to pause your game
to hurry over. Then there we are

side by side, looking out at the branches,
bent, outlined with ice, and intricate.

Single Again in Middle Age

I dredged a phrase up from my dream. I once dove
into the fire. The words flip-flop as the sky lightens.
Out of the . . . what? This morning, bleary at the stove,
cracking an egg, I've got the latter half about haplessly

conveying oneself from bad to worse, and can't recall
the beginning. I'd woken alarmed, bearing an urge
to caution a sensible young woman, poised to fall
as I had done. I'm now the wizened guide

flapping my red scarf. Her pretty, deaf ear turned
to friends (and me!), she sallies forth. What do I care?
Sunny-side up, sizzling in the butter. *I* learned
the hard way. Out of the lion's den? Out of the hailstorm?

Out of the downpour, the whirlwind, the bewitching kiss,
the beach camp's driftwood smoke, the braised sunset,
brazen lie, the bottomless abyss.
Salt, pepper, pinch of paprika. I concentrate

on the morning's good egg, nudge it onto the spatula,
ease it out of the frying pan, land it safely onto the plate.

My Son's Abandoned Aquarium

Three tropical fish swam up to feed on flakes
I sprinkled in. Face to the glass, searching
among their coral, their cave, their shipwreck,
I found the missing fourth, the smallest, color
of faded red marker, caught in the plastic grass.
I retrieved it with kitchen tongs, its tankmates
huddling behind the purple anemone.
Now what. People with your convictions,
I don't know what to do with a dead pet fish.
Easy enough to drop it—and the other three—
in the trash, be done. What makes me go
out to the yard, to scrape a hole with a rock,
place the thin shape in, and pat the earth down?

Your Husband

Your husband held the post office door for me
and yours flashed his lights at the intersection,
signaling for me to go first. Your husband
read the *Globe* sports section on the train, every
bit of it. We exchanged a look when a woman
two seats back answered her phone. Your husband
knelt in the plaza to tie his shoe, his backpack
slipping off his shoulder, a green apple escaping
from the unzipped pouch and landing at my feet.
In the lunch line ahead of me, your husband
ordered a Greek salad and at the last second
added a molasses cookie from the basket
by the register. Across the office at his desk,
your husband stretched his arms above his head,
arched his back, sighed, and returned his attention
to the screen. On the train home, your husband
played Candy Crush, his gym bag taking up
the space between us. I found your husband
puttering around the kitchen when I stopped in
to pick up my son. Offering a taste
of his home brew, he asked how I was doing.
I thought about it, and then pulled up a chair.

Now Approaching Porter Square

      On the Kendall Station platform,
I leave a dollar for the young woman
playing an accordion while stomping one foot
harnessed to a pulley that sets to dancing
her dressed-to-match marionette double
strung inside a suitcase box, one thin arm raised,
its painted red smile a fixed version
of the busking girl's real one.
      Trains running late, we pack in,
close enough to smell each other's leather
and perfume. *The arm belonged to Mrs. Danvers*,
I read from the book held open next to me,
clothbound, from the library, fitting
for the reader in a pink wool coat. *Last night I dreamt
I went to Manderley again.* I don't know whom
any of these arms belong to, nor these hands
holding devices, these shoulders slung with bags.
      As I grip the overhead strap, swaying
and steadying myself, my other hand dangles
empty, phoneless, bookless, ringless,
two inches from a stranger's. A firm hand,
long fingers, white shirt cuff. For a moment
I forget where I am, so strong
is my urge to slip my hand into that one,
as if it were familiar, as if it were
the most natural thing in the world.

Arrangements

One day the children got together
and put everybody back.

Back from their rentals,
their strange houses in other towns,
their second honeymoons.

Anna put her mother
on the sofa by the fire with the cat
and her father in the kitchen chopping vegetables,
radio tuned to the classical station. Between them
on the hall rug, Anna worked
making bead bracelets, red and green,
listening to French horns
swell through the house.

Ben, Ian, and the twins
put their parents in the big bed
and then they piled in with them
to be tickled and mussed with
though Ben thought he might be getting too old for that.

This was the long moment. For the children
the reunited parents behaved.
Anna's mother dug her hands deep into the cat's fur.
She felt nothing but a memory.

Their attention spans grew short.
And their days, in the scheme of things,
were numbered. Again,
they rearranged themselves.
This one with that one
and that one with this one.
For better or for worse

the children grew up
with this one, then with that one.

Boys on the Lake Dock

Racing out to the floating dock, freestyle,
the boys hoist themselves up, water dripping
from the bottoms of their swim shorts,

feet slapping the wooden boards.
How beautiful their backs, the arrows
of their shoulder blades and the twin dips

at their waistbands. The muscle and bone
of the boys, their scrapes and birthmarks,
smooth underarms. Backlit by the late sun.

Competing with their bodies now, diving,
cannon-balling, belly-flopping. Pretending
to be shot, falling stricken, sideways,

into the dark water, shouts swallowed,
coming up coughing. They're not the same.
The one kicks faster, dives straighter, executes

a double front-flip. All of it will always come
easier for him. There are those, aren't there?
The other kid's given up. Sprawled

on his back, one arm over his forehead
shading his eyes, he watches. As his friend
takes a running leap, swan diving

over him, the boy on the dock raises a leg
as if to bring his friend down from the sky.
Alone for a sweet moment after the splash.

Aerialist, Sixteen

Bands of heavy, colored fabric hang from the warehouse ceiling
    off Tank Farm Road. My niece comes here to climb them,
wrap herself in them, let them unwind, then knot and catch
    her falling body. To let them hold her in an arabesque high
above the ground. To be breathtaking. To astonish even herself.
    She's Wendy, learning to fly, learning what the body can do
and doing it, not yet understanding its power to affect.

The high school girl at the supermarket sings a Broadway tune,
    pierced, tattooed, as she scans my frozen lasagna.
She wants me to notice her clear, climbing voice,
    so I compliment her. She tells me she sings semi-professionally.
Keep it up, I encourage her, thinking of her making this declaration
    to each successive employer, each new lover, and then over the years
to her children, she will sing in the car, and tell them who she used to be.

The Wong-Baker FACES Pain Rating Scale

My son was remembering the faces he was asked to choose from when he had terrible leg pain. Days when he's not here, when he's with his dad, I eat out of a tuna-fish can standing at the counter. I stare blankly at his things, the evidence I didn't make him up. I don't drink. I'm not passed out in the driver's seat, but for him am I just as absent?

They're perfectly round, sort of man faces, the faces of a friendly man-moon. Drawn with only nine lines (if you count the line that makes the circle) from *no hurt* to *hurts little more*, then two lines forming eyelids for *hurts even more*, and four more lines to make tears for *hurts worst*. Four tears and the suggestion that the tears are flowing, falling off the face, one just making its way out of the eye on the left, the moon face's right eye, so the eyes are crying equally, two tears from the right eye, two from the left.

You wouldn't look at these faces and think, "These faces are supposed to be me." You would think, "This friendly moon man with a face that I feel comfortable looking at (sort of a cross between a face on a teddy bear and a face on a sugar cookie), this moon man is feeling this way, and it's ok that he's feeling this way, and I'm going to pick which of these ways it's ok that I'm feeling too."

But what if you pick incorrectly and then they give you the wrong treatment? What if you say *hurts worst* (because it really does hurt) but you don't actually know what *hurts worst* is because it's not like you were hit by a car on your bike, or got burned in a fire, or hadn't eaten anything but a few scoops of rice for many days. I only want to eat through whole packages or nothing at all.

To the Mother of the Family That Moved In

I moved on so you, unseen beauty, could get in.
What brought you? What do you feel
as you designate our emptied rooms?
Here for the silverware. Here for the tea tin.
Here for the Tiffany lamp. Also coats,
sheets, games, and your shoeboxes of photos.
Sweaters, I kept in the cedar closet.
I heard you have a dog. I placed a mat
at the bottom of the stairs so when mine
came skittering down, her old hips giving way,
she wouldn't slide into the hall table.
On her last day I carried her against my body
down from the sofa in my study (which was
the south room) and laid her on a blanket
in the back of my car. When I returned,
I sat by the attic-floor window. You will find
no one walking past below tends to look up.

Going up to Sleep in the Late Afternoon

Now I can see there were times when I took intense pleasure
and didn't know to name it.

I lie back on the bed. The echo of my body's shape surrounds me.
Sugar tree, untapped.

Funny how we say *took*, as if coming upon a finite source
and helping oneself.

The Joy Spell

If Christmas were for giving back,
think of our returns—

pilling sweaters, hateful words,
black-X'ed days on calendars.

The bullets from the children slain
retract into the killer's mother's gun.

What would fall into my lap?
That verbal slap I gave my son.

    *

Just past the ice cream stand, closed
for the season, a colored light display

spreads like a holiday apron
over a gray yard. In the misty rain

a man and boy move among wire cords,
arranging candy canes and elves.

Carloads of families will come by
to gaze as I do into the spell.

    *

My disposable cup proclaims JOY,
a sprinkled donut for the O.

The Shriners ring their bells.
New headlines. Same story.

Down the road Lucinda Williams sings,
You took my joy. I want it back.

"Here you are," I say to the radio,
and raise my cup.

Triolet for My Son

Sometimes you'll say, tell me a story—
one from your life I don't already know.
Then I'll trek to the border of memory
and summon another wayward story
to do with the girl named Amy.
She's soaring through the adagio,
shining from the second row. Tell me a story—
one from your life I don't already know.

Amy M. Clark is the author of the poetry collection *Stray Home* (University of North Texas Press, 2010), which was the 2009 winner of the Vassar Miller Prize in Poetry and a 2011 "Poetry Must-Read" selection by the Massachusetts Center for the Book. She is co-author with Molly Peacock of the chapbook *A Turn Around the Mansion Grounds: Poems in Conversation & a Conversation* (Slapering Hol Press, 2014). Her poems have been published in the anthologies *Good Poems, American Places* (Viking, 2011) and *Old Flame: from the First 10 Years of 32 Poems Magazine* (WordFarm, 2013), as well as many journals and magazines. She lives near Boston.

www.ingramcontent.com/pod-product-compliance
Lightning Source LLC
LaVergne TN
LVHW041345080426
835512LV00006B/629